Why This ROAD?

The Carolyn Myatt Story

2009-10 NMI MISSION EDUCATION RESOURCES

* * *

BOOKS

FROM MAIN STREET TO MANAGUA
Stories of Volunteer Missionaries
by Carol Anne Eby

MY BENGAL OF GOLD
The Church of the Nazarene in Bangladesh
by Dorli Gschwandtner

SMOKE THAT THUNDERS
Lessons from the Heart of Africa
by Gary D. Sidle

STRANGERS NO MORE
Welcoming Immigrants in North America
by Aimee Curtis

UNDER THE OMBU TREE
by Fletcher Tink

WHY THIS ROAD?
The Carolyn Myatt Story
by Betty Howard

* * *

ADULT MISSION EDUCATION LEADER'S RESOURCE PACKET

QUENCHING THE THIRST
Editors: Aimee Curtis and Rosanne Bolerjack

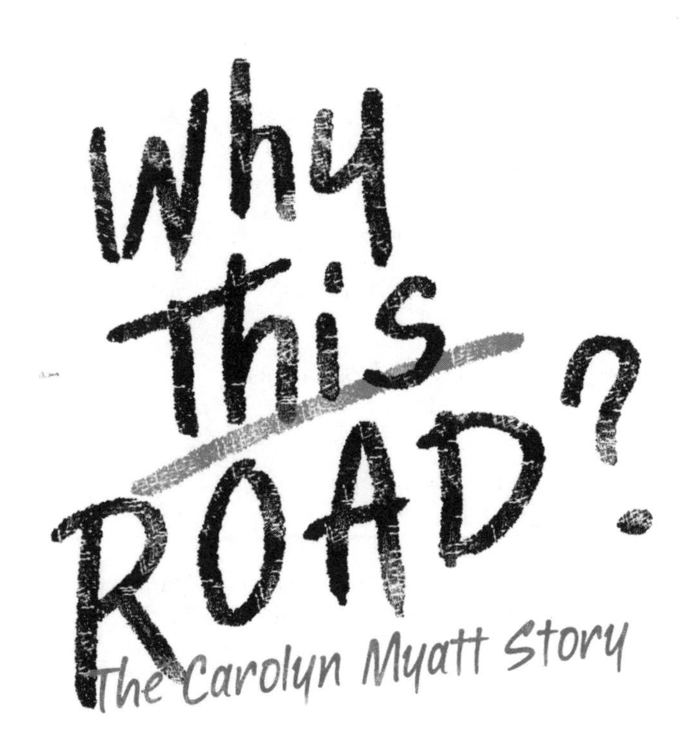

Nazarene Publishing House
Kansas City, Missouri

ISBN 978-0-8341-2420-2

Printed in the United States of America

Editor: Richard Buckner
Cover Design: Darlene Filley
Inside Design: Sharon Page

10 9 8 7 6 5 4 3 2 1

Acknowledgments

I wish to thank my granddaughter, Hannah Howard, for her invaluable assistance with copy-editing and proofreading this book.

Contents

BETTY HOWARD is retired, and she and her husband, John, live in Pensacola, Florida. She taught English several years; coauthored *World Within World Without,* a textbook for teaching college students literature from a Christian perspective; and retired after 12 years as editor of the quarterly devotional magazine *Daily Blessing.*

Betty has had a lifelong burden for global mission work, and her opportunity to participate firsthand came when her son and his family were called as missionaries to Kudjip Nazarene Hospital in Papua New Guinea. On a visit to her son and his family—Drs. Bob and Carol Howard and children, Hannah and Sam—she met missionary Carolyn Myatt. On following visits, as she observed Carolyn's work and the esteem with which she is held by Papua New Guineans, Betty realized Carolyn's story was one that would be a blessing to others. Nearly 10 years after she retired, Betty returned to the computer with the awareness that had guided her writing career found in a scripture she had kept taped to her computer: "My heart is inditing a good matter . . . my tongue is the pen of a ready writer" (Ps. 45:1, KJV).

Betty is originally from Oklahoma, where she received her bachelor's degree from the University of Tulsa and master's degree from Central State University at Edmond. She has taught a Sunday School class for many years, and the past four years she has assisted her son with an Adventurers group in Caravan at Ensley Church of the Nazarene in Pensacola.

Prologue

"I used to ask God to help me.
Then I asked God if I might help him.
I ended up by asking him
to do his work through me"
(James Hudson Taylor).

When Carolyn Myatt heard God's call, she responded with a total willingness to let God work through her. And He did so—dramatically. Through Carolyn, God transformed the health care and lives of people in two nations, all the while encouraging her and multiplying her talents many times over. Because Carolyn placed her full confidence in God and what He wanted her to do, her life became the remarkable story of courage and inspiration found in this book.

Many people have asked Carolyn how she knew God really wanted her to be a global missionary nurse. What gave her the assurance to forsake all and follow Him? This is the question most often asked about her years in India and Papua New Guinea. The answer, as Carolyn's story will show, speaks of God's sustaining love and the joy she experienced as He helped her accomplish more than she could have ever dreamed or imagined.

Carolyn was exceptionally qualified to serve as a missionary nurse. Graciously, God did not reveal the far-reaching scope of her call at the beginning, for it might have caused her great anxiety. In March 2000 Carolyn retired from being a global missionary for the Church of the Nazarene. She had served 29 years in India and 6 years in Papua New Guinea. Here is just a partial list of her many duties:

- Nurse and director of a mobile clinic that provided health care to Indian villages (1967-70)
- Tutor in the college of nursing at Reynolds Memorial (Nazarene) Hospital (1973-93)
- Mission treasurer for eight years (with colleague Jean Darling as her mentor)
- Hospital administrator of Reynolds Memorial Hospital (1980-92)
- Nurse anesthetist (1971-93)
- Providing hospitality in her home for hundreds of foreign and Indian guests who visited the hospital and college of nursing (1971-93)

- Envisioning and initiating the Community-Based Health Care (CBHC) program as an outreach health ministry from Reynolds Memorial Hospital (1984-90)

Following India's independence from Britain in 1947, a rising tide of militant Hinduism triggered a decision by Indian political leaders to deny new entry visas to non-Commonwealth applicants who were under assignment as replacements for retiring missionaries. Without replacements the government knew the missionary staff would decrease and eventually all missionaries would be eliminated. This decision accelerated the implementation of the Church of the Nazarene's policy to nationalize all ministries as quickly as possible. By 1993, Carolyn was the last Nazarene medical missionary in India.

The CBHC program Carolyn initiated had been so successful that mission leaders felt the program should be expanded into other world areas. In 1994 Carolyn was transferred to Papua New Guinea (PNG) for her last term of service with the mandate to begin a CBHC ministry there. Six years later, when Carolyn left PNG, the following advances had occurred:

- The CBHC program had been incorporated in 22 communities where 20,000 people lived at a cost of $16 to $20 for a lifetime of preventive health care.
- One thousand people in the 22 communities had been trained to give leadership in their own CBHC program and to act as "health experts."
- Six training manuals for the CBHC program had been written and published.
- The PNG Department of Health had adopted the Nazarene CBHC as a model for the PNG nation.
- Grants from various funding agencies totaling almost 2 million dollars had been received or were in the pipeline to finance the CBHC program.
- Hundreds of people in 22 communities had accepted Jesus as their Savior because village leaders accepted the challenge to evangelize their communities.
- New Nazarene churches had been established in some of the 22 communities.

Is it any wonder that the name Carolyn Myatt is esteemed in India and PNG? Ken Silvers—a

Nazarene layman from the Chicago Central District who has been involved in Nazarene Missions International many years and had visited Carolyn in India—said, "The Catholics have their Mother Teresa. The Nazarenes have Carolyn." This was a sentiment echoed by Mother Teresa herself in a letter to Carolyn expressing her appreciation for the nursing education Reynolds Memorial Hospital's nursing college provided for young ladies who were considering joining her Missionaries of Charity order of nuns.

1

A Dream Come True

"Sometimes when people speak, their words are so strong and go so deep they seem to have a quality of eternity about them" (Thomas Moore).

There was a nip in the air, and the flame-colored leaves on the maples and oaks rustled in the breeze as Carolyn and Beverly Beeler hurried across the campus at Eastern Nazarene College that fall day in 1957. They were on their way to the dining hall for their lunch—and a date with destiny. Carolyn and Beverly sat opposite each other near the center of the dining area, which gave each of them a good view of about half the students in the room. Carolyn noticed how young some of them looked—a detail she was well aware of, since she was entering college late after having completed her training to become a registered nurse. Her sister's attention, however, was on something entirely different.

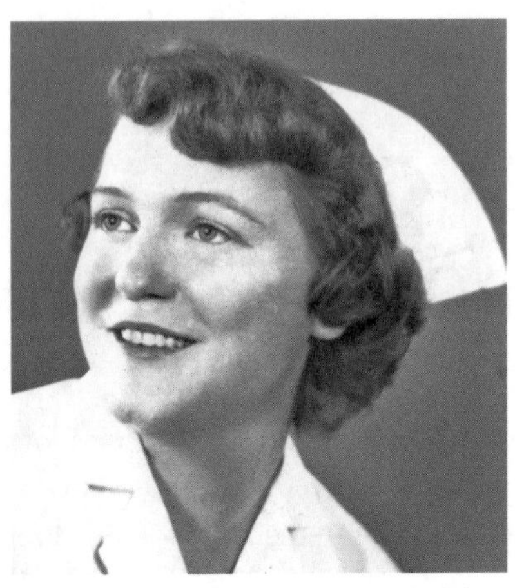

Carolyn graduating from nursing school in 1957

"Don't look now," Beverly whispered, "but there's the cutest guy standing over by the back door. I'll tell you when you can look." Suspense mounted as Carolyn waited for the go-ahead signal from her sister.

"You can look now," Beverly finally whispered. Carolyn turned around and had her "lookfull." Sure enough, her sister had not exaggerated one bit. The young man was handsome indeed. He was not only attractive but also dignified, and she knew at once that he was someone she would like to meet.

Carolyn soon got acquainted with Russell Myatt and began to date him. The better she knew him, the more she liked him. Russ, who was from Canada, had received a bachelor of arts degree and was working on a theology degree. He had already gained admission to Nazarene Theological Seminary to continue his theological education. Russ was working his way through college, so their limited time together was spent on study dates in the library. That was all right with Carolyn, for it was soon obvious that this was likely to be a "till death do us part" relationship.

It was not a surprise when Russ asked Carolyn to marry him at Christmas. They planned to be married in June and then head for Kansas City and seminary. Becoming a minister's wife would be a natural fit for Carolyn. While she was growing up, she and her family attended their church's every service. She sometimes fell asleep in the pew, but she was raised believing that going to church and serving God were important.

Carolyn accepted the Lord as her Savior when she was 12 years old. A short time later the pastor's son, whom she did not know, came to preach in her church. After the service was over, the speaker walked down the aisle toward Carolyn. Members of the congregation crowded around him trying to greet him, but he kept moving down the aisle until he reached her pew.

"Little girl," he said as he looked intently into Carolyn's eyes, "you were my inspiration today." Through this young minister God may have been hinting to Carolyn about the special work He had in store for her.

One of Carolyn's childhood dreams, like most girls, was to have a big, formal, church wedding. She knew her family could not provide it for her, because she was one of seven children whom her parents struggled to support during the Great Depression of the 1930s. Her father worked for a utility company in the gas fields of Pennsylvania, and her mother was a practical nurse. Their income did not include money for frills, such as their daughter's dream wedding. But Carolyn had an idea!

Since she was already certified as a registered nurse, she told Russ she wanted to return home and work as a staff nurse so she could save money for their wedding. He had no objection; after all, he had a tough semester ahead. His time would be filled studying for his theology degree and working at two jobs to pay for his education and living expenses. He knew their time together would be limited even if they were both on campus.

Carolyn returned to her parents' home in Washington, Pennsylvania, and got a job at the local hospital until school was out. Days flew by as she, along with her mother and sisters, worked feverishly on the details of the wedding. It was an exciting time for the whole family.

Then one beautiful sunny day in June, Carolyn had the wedding of her dreams. Her father

Russell and Carolyn Myatt on their way to the reception after their wedding ceremony

walked down the aisle with Carolyn on his arm. Russ's father, a Nazarene preacher, performed the ceremony. Five bridesmaids stood beside her, along with a flower girl and a ring bearer. Her brother Bill sang "Savior, like a Shepherd Lead Us" while Russ and Carolyn knelt and took Communion together for the first time as husband and wife. Everything was perfect!

Russ was firm in his belief that although the bride's family paid for most of the wedding expenses, the honeymoon should be his expense alone—even though he had limited funds. Tuition and other college expenses had taken most of his savings. Russ considered several possible honeymoon sites and soon concluded that the only place he could afford was located in northern Pennsylvania. Their honeymoon location was to be a camping site in Cook State Park.

When they arrived at the park on Saturday after the wedding, they found the recreational area more picturesque than they had imagined. Their "spartanly adequate" cabin was near a beautiful natural-basin swimming pool. A little stream ran through the area, and deer could be seen running free through the forest. In fact, the campsite proprietor told the newlyweds when they arrived that bear had recently been seen in the area. They were not alarmed by this news; it just made their honeymoon site all that more special.

There was one drawback. The cabins didn't have attached bathrooms. The only rest rooms were located near the swimming pool. To get to them, guests had to walk over a narrow footbridge or cross a rustic car bridge made of wide, wooden planks. The placement of the rest rooms seemed to be only a minor inconvenience.

On Sunday they attended a nearby Nazarene church. Even though Russ was from Canada, someone in the congregation knew him and asked him to give his testimony during the service. One of the things he said that day replayed in Carolyn's mind countless times in the days that followed. "I don't know what tomorrow holds, but I know Who holds tomorrow," Russ affirmed with a glowing face.

On Monday it rained all day and all night. Tuesday produced even more rain. The stream that ran through the campsite overflowed its banks. Wednesday morning it was still raining, and the rising torrents of water swirled just below the level of the car bridge. Beyond the bridge the frigid water flooded into the natural-basin swimming pool until it reached a depth of about 12 feet. Wednesday afternoon the rain abated, none too soon for the bridal couple.

When the rain ceased, Russ and Carolyn were able to get out and do some of the things they had planned before the downpour. However, by Thursday evening Carolyn did not feel well. Ever since she had endured a childhood bout of rheumatic fever, her joints would occasionally ache, especially when it rained. That day, besides aching joints, she also had a headache. So at about 7:30 in the evening she decided to lie down on the bed to rest. Her attentive bridegroom brought a cool washcloth and placed it across her forehead.

Around 8:45 Russ bent down and whispered in her ear, "I'm going across to the rest room. The keys are in my pocket. You can unlock the door if you want to go out, but no one can come in while I'm gone." She couldn't remember later if she had answered him. She only remembered hearing his footsteps go off the porch of the cabin. Apparently she fell asleep immediately.

2
Everything Changed

"Sometimes, in the midst of a family, without warning of a gathering storm . . . will fall a terrible fact, and from that moment everything is changed. The air is thick with cloud; and cannot weep itself clean" (George McDonald).

Carolyn awakened around two o'clock in the morning. All was very, very quiet in the darkened cabin. Carolyn bolted upright in bed when she realized she was still dressed in her skirt and blouse, immediately sensing that something was wrong. Her heart pounded as she turned on the bedside lamp.

Russ? Where is Russ?

Terror gripped her as she remembered clearly the events of the early evening hours. Recalling every word that Russ had whispered in her ear hours before, she rushed out into the cold, dark night and began to cry out as loudly as her trembling voice would allow, "Russ, Russ!" But the only sound she heard was her own voice echoing eerily from the surrounding mountains.

Frantically she started running down the wet gravel road toward the rest rooms that were illuminated by a single electric lightbulb attached to the outside of the building. As she ran toward the light, her mind was flooded with possibilities of what might have happened to keep Russ from returning. *Perhaps a bear has attacked and dragged Russ into the woods,* was her first thought. But wouldn't someone have heard cries from such an attack?

No, most likely his absence is associated with the water, she concluded, as she pictured Russ trudging across that same slippery footbridge hours earlier to reach the rest rooms. The stream had receded, but the water in the swimming pool was still quite deep. The most hopeful scenario she could think of was that he had received an injury of some kind. Perhaps Russ had fallen and struck his head or broken a bone.

Fortunately the light on the rest rooms illuminated the footbridge just enough for her to see to make her way across it. She rushed to the men's side of the building and pushed open the door. It was empty! She then checked the women's side, and it, too, was empty. As she stood there, confused about what to do next, it felt, she later recalled, as if evil hands reached out from the darkness, crushing her chest until she gasped for breath. She had never felt such absolute terror as that gripping her at that moment!

Since all the campers had been confined to their cabins by the rain, the couple had not gotten to know anyone at the campsite. Fortunately Carolyn remembered that some college girls were staying in a cabin nearby, so she hurried to their door and began knocking frantically. There was no response.

Even in her state of terror she realized that college girls alone in a cabin in a remote area had reason to be afraid of opening their door in the middle of the night. She began telling them her urgent problem through the locked door. The panic in her voice apparently convinced the girls she meant them no harm. They cautiously opened the door. She asked if they would walk with her to the park office so she could telephone her parents. They quickly dressed and the five of them walked toward the office. Fortunately, one of the girls had brought a flashlight. "Will you flash the light over there on the water?" Carolyn said to the girl holding the flashlight, motioning toward the swimming pool as they walked across the car bridge.

"Lady, don't even be thinking those things," was her response. "Your husband is all right." Although reluctant, she honored Carolyn's request and shined the light out across the dark water. They could see nothing.

When Carolyn arrived at the office, she explained to the park manager that her husband was missing. She asked permission to use the telephone to notify the police and her parents. The manager had the same attitude as that of the girl holding the flashlight, and she refused to allow Carolyn to use the phone.

"Your husband will be found soon and he will be embarrassed if he finds you have alarmed people needlessly," she said. But she assured Carolyn she would notify the local authorities.

"You girls go on back to this lady's cabin and keep her company until we find her husband," she said to the college girls.

While the girls huddled around the table in the cabin, Carolyn sat on the bed with her heart breaking. At first the girls spoke in whispers, but after a while they became more conversational, discussing lighthearted topics typical of college girls. Carolyn realized these young ladies were in a situation that even most mature adults would find challenging to respond to appropriately.

At 4:30 in the morning Carolyn, accompanied by the college students, went back to the park office and insisted she be permitted to call her parents. Her stunned parents said they would leave immediately for the park.

When Carolyn's parents arrived several hours later, she told them she believed Russ had drowned. The three of them soon began walking out toward the car bridge.

The state police were already on-site, and a search party of men soon arrived. Some of them branched out into the nearby wooded areas, while others began removing the wooden planks at the end of the swimming pool so the water level would go down. One man wearing hip boots stood in the pool directly across from the bridge where Carolyn and her parents were standing. While her dad cradled her in his arms, the three of them watched as the man, carrying a large hook-like implement in his hand, waded through the deep, cloudy water of the pool toward them. They watched the man approach and saw him toss the hook into the water. Then Carolyn stood aghast as she realized the hook had caught on something.

"Here he is!" the man shouted.

Carolyn gasped as she saw a piece of the blue sweater Russ had been wearing pulled above the surface of the water.

3
The Call

"To the dead he sayeth: Arise!
To the living follow me!
And the voice soundeth on
From the centuries that are gone
To the centuries that shall be"
(Henry Wadsworth Longfellow).

During the exhausting days prior to Russ's funeral, Carolyn felt wrapped in a cocoon of love as her family and church friends ministered to her in a multitude of ways. But there seemed to be no source, either human or divine, that could diminish the deep sadness that permeated her innermost being. Her employer before she resigned to get married, Washington Hospital and its nursing authorities, quickly assured Carolyn she could have her job back. Furthermore, if she wished, she could be assigned to work in another area of nursing. Carolyn told them she would like to work in the pediatric department.

At the time of Russ's death Carolyn was unaware of any information available about the stages of grief to be bridged following the death of a loved one. She simply knew she had intolerable pain. There seemed to be no real help coming from her well-meaning family and friends—such as the trusted friend from college who wrote her words of sympathy and concluded with the well-meaning admonition, "Carolyn, don't ask God why." But she did ask God why. Every anguished cry of Carolyn's heart at this time seemed to begin with why.

"Why, Lord? Why Russ, Lord? Why me, Lord?"

As time passed, Carolyn buried herself in her pediatric nursing career. All of her emotional upheaval was muted during the hours she was on duty. Church attendance was the exact opposite. People at church seemed to have moved on with their lives while Carolyn continued to feel engulfed by grief. So after 23 years of faithful attendance, Carolyn quit going to church. She simply could not reconcile what had transpired in her life with the teaching of Scripture that we have a loving Savior. Every day she felt more and more isolated. Her response was to strike out at everything that was part of her normal experience, including her parents.

Don't they understand that life for me can never again be normal? Carolyn thought each time her parents said something that sounded as if they expected her to continue with life as usual. She knew her refusal to attend church would be painful for her parents, but she believed she had to shield herself from the emotional turmoil she felt in that setting.

"Are you going to church today?" Carolyn's father asked one morning when it became clear she was not getting ready.

"No," Carolyn replied that morning and every Sunday thereafter when he asked her the same question. She usually added such statements as "Leave me alone!" "The Bible is not true!" and "God is not love!"

"You can refuse to go with me, but I will always ask," was her father's response again and again.

The long, lonely hours she chose to spend in her room gave Carolyn time to reflect on her childhood, as well as the tragedy that had turned her life upside down. She thought back to the time when she was 10 years old and had spent long days in another room following the prescribed treatment for rheumatic fever. It was during this time of enforced bed rest that Carolyn felt she should go into nursing. Some questioned her ability to pursue such a physically demanding career, assuming that a rheumatic fever diagnosis was synonymous with heart damage. When the time came for Carolyn to apply for nurse's training, however, her family doctor who had cared for her during her illness was the examining physician. He knew she had no heart involvement and immediately approved her admission to the school of nursing.

Each time Carolyn relived the details of her life leading up to that tragic fifth night of her honeymoon, the question "Why?" flooded her mind, and each time she entertained that thought, she felt great guilt. Eventually she began to feel extremely hypocritical and unspiritual. True Christians should not question God's will, right? She did not realize until much later that while God's sinless Son hung on the Cross, He also asked His Father, "Why have you forsaken me?"

"Will you go to church with us this morning?"

Carolyn's father asked again one morning as he had every Sunday for many months. This time he added, "We are holding revival meetings and our evangelist is a well-known preacher from the East Coast." Carolyn viewed this invitation with suspicion. Reluctantly she agreed to accompany her parents later in the week, with the understanding that everyone at church would leave her alone. She had no reason to worry, for few if any at church would have approached her anyway. She'd had such a chip on her shoulder for so long that most of the people stayed a safe distance from her.

Carolyn attended the last revival service on Sunday evening. After the service the evangelist asked Carolyn if he could come to her home the next day to talk to her. She couldn't think of a way to get out of it, since her parents had told him she would be off work for the day.

When the evangelist arrived at Carolyn's home, he made a strange request: "Can we go to the cemetery where your husband is buried?" Her warped thinking went into high gear. *Not at church, not at home, but at the cemetery! I'm really going to hear it for the way I've shut out people so long, especially church people.*

When they arrived at the cemetery, the evangelist asked Carolyn's mother and the wife of their pastor who had accompanied them to allow him to have some time alone with Carolyn.

"You know, Carolyn, there are things worse than death," the evangelist said as he looked down at the granite headstone that marked Russ's grave. He went on to tell her about his wife, who was confined in a mental institution with catatonic schizophrenia. Carolyn had taken care of patients with that problem, and his statement brought back mental images of people sitting rigidly on chairs staring into space, unable to communicate with others. Perhaps there was something worse than death—a living death, Carolyn acknowledged to herself.

"Some people have given up on you," the evangelist went on to say. "But I have all the confidence in the world God will redeem you to himself." It was the first time in three years that someone had expressed confidence in Carolyn's ability to move beyond the prolonged grief that had engulfed her.

Not long after the conversation with the evangelist, Carolyn was visiting a cousin who made a simple offer that was to have a profound effect on her life: "I have a copy of the book *To Live Again* by Catherine Marshall. Would you like to read it?"

The book appealed to Carolyn because she strongly identified with the writer, who also had lost her minister husband at a youthful age. As she began to read about Catherine Marshall's struggle following her husband's death, God spoke to her heart and she began to believe once again that God is a God of love. She asked God to forgive her and was, indeed, "redeemed to himself" just as the evangelist had predicted.

While Carolyn was struggling with her relationship with the Lord, her mother must have been quite surprised one day when Carolyn told her about a recurrent dream she had experienced. In it she saw a large crowd of people walking down a road. They would come to a cliff and tumble over it. One day she said an astonishing thing to her mother, considering how she was acting at the time: "I think God is calling me to the mission field." Her mother was so taken aback by this statement that her only response was, "Oh?"

Carolyn prayed a lot after coming back to the Lord, and she told Him one day, "If You want me to go to a foreign field, I'm ready. But I don't want this to be a reaction to my tragedy. If You want me to go, make it very plain." Then she got even more specific—something she says she would not recommend others to do: "Hit me over the head with a call, and I'll go," she prayed.

One evening at about six o'clock her pastor's wife called. "We are on our way to the Monongahela Nazarene Church," she said. "Dr. Howard Hamlin, a missionary surgeon from our Nazarene hospital in Swaziland, Africa, is speaking. We wondered if you would like to go along?"

"What time does the service start?" Carolyn asked.

"We can make it if we leave immediately," she replied.

"Just go on without me," Carolyn told her. "I don't have time to get ready; and besides I had a very exhausting day at the hospital."

"No," her pastor's wife said. "We'll just wait for you."

How could Carolyn refuse to go? She quickly changed her clothes, and they sped to the church 17 miles away. They arrived after the service had begun, and the sanctuary was quite full. Chagrined, Carolyn had to trudge down the aisle to sit in the second row! Dr. Hamlin soon was telling about his experiences in Africa. In the midst of telling one story, even though he was using normal speaking tones, these words stood out for Carolyn: "And the old African chieftain told me to come home and tell you we need doctors and nurses." *I'm sure there must be a great need for missionary doctors and nurses,* Carolyn acknowledged silently.

A few moments later, Dr. Hamlin, who was an excellent speaker, said in a more emphatic tone: "And the old African chieftain told me to come home and tell you we need doctors and nurses!"

At that precise moment Carolyn had an assurance deep within her spirit that this was the call of God. She knew that as a nurse she could fulfill that need. She had been praying that God would leave no doubt in her mind about her being a "called-out one." In fact, it had just been a few weeks since she had told the Lord to "hit me over the head with the call so I will know it is You."

Carolyn found herself praying with new intensity: "Lord, if this is really You and You are speaking to me—if You are really calling me—make me certain that it is Your call." A couple of minutes later Dr. Hamlin said a third time and even louder, "And the old African chieftain told me to come home and tell you we need doctors and nurses!" Immediately Carolyn said yes in her heart.

At the end of the service Dr. Hamlin invited those to come forward who would be willing to answer God's call to missionary service if He should call them. Carolyn immediately stood to her feet and walked to the altar. Her district superintendent, Reverend R. Beverly Acheson, who was in the service, was aware of her spiritual struggle. He walked down from the platform to the altar and asked Carolyn, "Do you mean it?" "Yes, I do," she assured him. "Then see me right after the service," he said. "I must tell you something."

At the end of the service he told her: "I think you should know that when Dr. Hamlin and I were praying for the service tonight, God showed me that you would be here and that you would answer the call." God had confirmed His calling on her life through another—this one whom she admired and respected.

When Carolyn went home from the service bubbling in her heart and told her mom and dad that she had said yes to God's call, she noticed her dad was very quiet; but she didn't suspect his reaction was anything other than the normal response of a father relinquishing his child for missionary service.

4

A Change of Heart

"Sometimes God disturbs the water before sending his healing angel" (John Harper).

Carolyn applied to the Nazarene World Missions Department and began the formal application process in 1963. She fully expected to be sent to Africa if her application were to be accepted. But in 1965 when her appointment as a foreign missionary nurse came, it was to India, not Africa.

"Carolyn, let's go into the kitchen and have a cup of coffee," her father said one cold day when he was helping her pack her crates. "I'm helping you get ready to leave for India, but I can't keep it a secret any longer. I don't want you to go." He went on to say, "In fact, I feel so strongly about it that if it were possible, I would take back my promises to God that I made when you were dedicated as a baby."

Caught off guard by his statement, Carolyn could only reply, "This is just something you will have to deal with God about. I must go."

Carolyn continued with her packing and also began making preparations to attend an orientation workshop for global missionaries who would soon be departing for their first assignment. The meeting was held at Bethany Nazarene College (now Southern Nazarene University) in Bethany, Oklahoma.

On the first day of the workshop Carolyn was excited to meet many interesting people and gain insights she was sure would be helpful.

On the evening of the second day of the conference, though, Carolyn had a piercing headache that just wouldn't go away. The next morning she began to stagger and weave from side to side. She had to shield her eyes in brightly lit rooms and even had a short period of blindness. Nausea, vomiting, and a low-grade fever that followed made her feel even more wretched. She knew these symptoms could be associated with serious illnesses of the nervous system and the brain. As soon as seminar leaders became aware of Carolyn's symptoms, they whisked her away to a nearby hospital emergency room. Dr. Dudley Powers, a Nazarene physician, examined Carolyn and admitted her to an isolation room. A short time later he came into the room and made a startling statement: "Carolyn, I'm sorry to have to tell you this. You have viral encephalitis."

Apparently not surprised to hear this grim diagnosis, Carolyn's only response in a weak voice was, "Dr. Powers, I need to use a telephone. I must call my dad."

"You can't do that!" he said, "You're too weak."

Finally, after a passionate, tearful plea, the doctor had a telephone brought to her bedside.

It was late Sunday afternoon when Carolyn finally reached her dad. He and her mom were getting ready to go to the evening church service. She reported to her father the things the doctor had told her.

"There are three possible outcomes for me with this diagnosis," she told her concerned father. "No. 1, I can get better with no aftereffects. No. 2, I can live but have brain damage. And No. 3, I can die. But no matter which of these happens, it is all right. If the outcome is negative, Dad, I don't want you to have any bitterness about it."

Carolyn's dad relayed the conversation to her mother and asked her to dress quickly because he wanted to get to the church as soon as possible. When the couple arrived at the church, the first thing Carolyn's father did was request that the pastor's wife represent his daughter and be anointed for her healing. The pastor's wife later shared that as she knelt at the altar and had her head anointed with oil, she felt sure Carolyn was going to die. After the prayer time was over, she got up from her knees and went immediately to an empty classroom where she again dropped to her knees and began to pray.

Consternation overtook her when an image of Carolyn's father's face flashed before her eyes.

"I'm praying for Carolyn, not her father," she reminded the Lord. Her protestation was useless. She continued to see Mr. Beeler's face and not Carolyn's.

When the imagery persisted, she went to the back of the sanctuary where Carolyn's father was seated. She beckoned him to come outside and confronted him:

"Mr. Beeler, every time I pray for Carolyn, I see your face. Do you know what this is all about?"

"I certainly do," Mr. Beeler said. "God has

shown me that if He wants Carolyn, He can simply take her rather than taking her to India. If I can have a little time at the end of the service, I want to confess my sin to God and to the church."

At the end of the service, Carolyn's father walked to the front of the church and confessed his sin to God and to the congregation. Meanwhile, that night in Bethany, Oklahoma, Carolyn's fever fell. Five days later she flew home to Pennsylvania, unaccompanied. One month later she left for India with the blessing of her father.

5

Learning to Trust

"Nothing strengthens us as much as isolation and transplantation; because under this wholesome demand, the soul will put forth all its native vigor" (F. D. Meyer).

Carolyn departed for India in a whirlwind of compassion and affirmation. She flew first to England and continued her journey on an Orient and Pacific ship, sailing through the vibrant blue waters of the Mediterranean Sea and the Suez Canal and into the Arabian Sea. She enjoyed the fellowship of the four other Nazarene missionaries who were on board the ship. Carolyn and two others disembarked in Bombay on October 27, 1965. Two of the missionaries continued on their way to Papua New Guinea, an island nation north of Australia.

When Carolyn arrived in the land of her calling, the words of General Superintendent G. B. Williamson at the beautiful sending ceremony for the missionaries being commissioned were still ringing in her ears: "Your call will sustain you!"

Perhaps this assurance, along with an article she read on board ship titled, "Why Foreign Postings Don't Work," foreshadowed what was to come. The information in this article was gleaned from Western diplomatic and military personnel. The article basically concluded that Western personnel living in third world countries do not stay unless their environment is altered sufficiently to make it more like their own.

In order to minimize the impact of cross-cultural living for newly appointed missionaries, the Nazarene leadership had attempted to familiarize them with the stages of cultural adjustment they would likely encounter. First, they were told, there would be the stage of fascination similar to the feelings a tourist experiences. This would deteriorate into the stage of rejection, which would be followed by the minimal-adjustment stage. Finally, if they lasted through these three stages, they would reach their goal of cultural adjustment. They, then, would be able to function effectively as global missionaries.

Carolyn soon concurred with the mission leadership's analysis that while "cross-cultural visiting" is glamorous, "cross-cultural living" is an entirely different story. There she was, in the land of her adoption, unquestionably due to the bidding of God, and she was eager to get started. However, she soon found that a call from God does not mean straight-ahead, smooth sailing and special privileges. Indeed, cross-cultural living is one of the most challenging adjustments a person can make.

Carolyn had complete assurance that God had called her to go to India and felt confident she would not be overwhelmed by culture shock; however, she almost failed to make it through the second stage. As time went by, disenchantment with India set in—generally at first and more specifically with her people and their customs.

Moreover, the things in her previous living environment that had given her self-identity and self-esteem had been altered or taken away completely. The props, as she called them, which had given meaning to her life, were no longer present. She felt very isolated.

For Carolyn the props included her loving and supportive family. They were thousands of miles away. There was no daily or even weekly contact. Yes, they corresponded, but it took two weeks for letters to get to her parents and two weeks to receive a response. Telephone calls, except to and from Bombay, were impossible.

Another prop that was compromised for Carolyn was her ability to express herself adequately. The simplest Marathi phrases threw her. She sputtered and stammered when she attempted to speak, so she spent a lot of her time smiling and saying "salaam" (hello) or "ki?" which is simply the one-word question "What?" She had always found learning easy, but learning the Marathi language was quite difficult. Marathi does not use the English alphabet; instead it is written in a phonetic script called Balbodh. But even if she mastered the Marathi language, it was only one of 14 major languages the people of India spoke.

She also had to adopt the Indian Nazarenes' worship style. What a big change that was! She had to listen to Scripture and prayers in the Marathi language. She found it uncomfortable to sit cross-legged on the floor during Sunday worship time, and the music sounded eerie to her Western ears.

Then there were the problems associated with food and eating. Indians eat with their fingers. The first time Carolyn tried this, juices dripped off her elbows causing the people sitting around her to laugh. Just the smell of the spices nauseated her. And when she ate food containing the unfamiliar peppery spices, her nose dripped, her lips felt numb, or she would later have diarrhea.

The temperature in Central India was hot, hotter, and hottest—110 to 120 degrees Fahrenheit during the summer season (mid-February to mid-June). It was so hot that for many years it was considered unsafe for missionaries to live on the central plains during the summer months. So they, along with affluent Indians and Europeans living there, sought refuge in areas with a higher elevation. Carolyn chose to vacation in the Himalayan foothills at about 7,000 feet above sea level.

Carolyn's shopping area for major purchases was 400 miles away in Bombay. She traveled by a train that was constantly packed to unsafe limits. Many disappointed travelers were always left standing forlornly on the railway platform when the train pulled out. The trip to Bombay was an overnight journey of 12 hours.

Carolyn's home did not have a water-heating system. She used cold water whenever possible.

To wash dishes or take a bath, she heated water on the stove and carried it to where she needed it. Drinking water had to be boiled for 20 minutes to make it safe. Milk from a water buffalo was brought to her door in a small aluminum jug. She strained the milk through a thin cloth to remove the ever-present debris. Then she boiled it to pasteurize it. If she wanted bread, she had to buy the wheat grain, send it to a mill to be ground into flour, and finally make the bread and bake it.

There was a taboo against beef in India, since Indian Hindus consider cows sacred. If Carolyn wanted beef, she had to call the Muslim butcher to bring it. He would carry a few chunks of meat inside a burlap bag and then hide behind her garden wall. From there he would send a message saying, "The man with the red vegetables is here."

Carolyn was in language study the first two years she was in India and had to set aside her nursing career. When at last she began to practice nursing, she found this was difficult also. The supplies and equipment she considered necessary to practice her profession weren't available. Furthermore, she soon learned she was in a land where nurses were not revered. In India nursing was considered a dirty, immoral occupation because nurses touched the bodies of men who were not their family members—a strict taboo in India.

During language study Carolyn lived in a large house, interestingly called a bungalow, with 14 evangelical missionaries from other denominations or organizations. Every one of them felt confident about having been called by God; but for each of them the fascination for India that was felt at first eventually descended the ladder to rejection. Every bull session ended with this conclusion: India will never change, and unless India changes there will be no progress. Eleven of the 14 missionaries made it through only one term of service. After five years, only 3 of the 14 remained in India for a second term.

Oh, the disenchantment Carolyn felt. She did not like India, and she did not like her people! She began to wonder, *Can I minister effectively to these people when I don't like them or their ways?*

Carolyn felt hypocritical, but she knew that if she left India, she would be considered a failure by many. Spiritual lassitude also set in. In her feeble prayers she was continually petitioning God for some kind of a miracle that would deliver her from the absence of peace within her heart. Then, in what seemed to be a stroke of good fortune, the armies of India and Pakistan massed on the border between these two countries and war began. It was bandied about that foreigners would have to leave India. The Indian Christians were distressed about both the war and what appeared to be the imminent departure of the missionaries; but in Carolyn's heart she was saying, *Goody, goody, goody. I'm going to get to leave India and no one will know I was a failure!*

Unfortunately, Carolyn's elation was short-lived. A truce between the two countries was declared, and for Carolyn things went from bad to worse. She was struggling desperately. One Sunday morning as she traveled to church in a rickshaw, she poured out her heart to God: "Lord, somehow make this day special for me. If You don't, I'll have to leave India." Her mind had become so confused that she wasn't even sure at that moment if her prayer was sincere. But God saw the desperation of Carolyn's heart that morning, and something special happened. Carolyn shares:

> In an overwhelming experience of God's grace, His Spirit reached out through that

murky gloom and touched my heart and my innermost being. He did it by changing me, not my circumstances. India remained the same, but I had been changed. Almighty God met me in a truly mountaintop experience. However powerful that experience was, I cannot dwell on it. The important thing was the changes He instantly made in me. At that moment God poured His love for India and her people into my heart. India became my home. I knew from that moment on I was God's instrument in India.

6

India at Grassroots Level

"A Christian should always remember that the value of his good works is not based on their number and excellence, but on the love of God that prompts him to do these things" (John of the Cross).

At the time Carolyn went to India, Nazarene work was located at the center of the subcontinent if you measure north to south and east to west at the Bombay-Calcutta latitude. After Carolyn completed her first assignment, which was to learn the language, she was assigned to the mobile health unit of Reynolds Memorial (Nazarene) Hospital at Washim, Maharashtra State. Most Americans would have felt uneasy and uncomfortable in this hospital, for it was rugged and minimally equipped, but Indian patients considered it luxurious.

The mobile health unit was located in the town of Buldana on the western edge of the Church of the Nazarene district. The mobile unit's staff visited specific villages and offered health services to the people of the surrounding area. This assignment enabled Carolyn to see India at a grassroots level—to observe firsthand the plight of the people. This was invaluable preparation for the work God had in store for her that one day would change the face of health care in two countries.

Carolyn witnessed the distressing living conditions of Indian people as she traveled through the large cities. She observed people living in hovels with gunnysacks for doors. She saw them living in windowless shacks along the lanes, footpaths, and railroad tracks. Once they had dared to dream these cities held the key to unlock the vicious cycle of poverty and hunger for them and their families. Instead, they experienced the hideous nightmare of a hostile city where social injustices and manipulation of the poor by the rich were the norm.

When she traveled into the countryside with the mobile health-care unit, Carolyn saw a different but equally tragic picture. People worked long hours in the fields of wealthy landowners for a pittance. An undernourished mother unable to breastfeed her baby would work all day squatting down or bending over in the fields just to get enough money to buy a quart of milk. Or most likely she would purchase only half as much and dilute it with equal portions of water. The rest of the family would get a little more to eat, but the infant would cry himself to sleep. The malnutrition/disease sequence would likely begin, and without some intervention, the baby would be the one child out of four to die before reaching four years of age.

Carolyn was heartbroken when she saw the crowds of sick people seeking the help of doctors and traditional healers to treat their many commonplace diseases. Safe water and a better understanding of hygiene and the causes of these diseases could have prevented them. She concluded that ignorance itself was one of the most insidious forces that kept the people mired in an environment that made them susceptible to disease. She saw how desperately they needed hope—hope that dreaded diseases such as tuberculosis, leprosy, typhoid fever, diarrhea, and dysentery could be eliminated as a common problem facing their community.

By God's grace and His special touch Carolyn was able to minister effectively despite the challenge of cross-cultural adjustments. Not only did she and her team provide health care that improved the daily lives of the people, they also loved the people unconditionally and gave them the liberating message of life in Christ.

On completion of her assignment with the mobile health unit, Carolyn was asked to serve as the last expatriate director of nursing at Reynolds Memorial Hospital. After Carolyn, this responsibility would go to Nalini Yangad, an Indian national whose parents had been among the early converts in India. Carolyn was also the mission treasurer, serving in this role for eight years along with her other assignments. Colleague Jean Darling was her mentor.

During Carolyn's service in India, Reynolds Memorial was a 105-bed facility that included a school of nursing for general nursing and midwifery. In a typical year the hospital staff treated 36,000 outpatients and 4,500 in-patients, performed 800 operations, and delivered 1,000 babies. It employed more than a hundred people—doctors, nurses, laboratory technicians, X-ray technicians, business personnel, cleaners, and so on. In addition, it had about 40 nursing students at any given time. With the exception of Esther Howard, a graduate from Samaritan Hospital in

Nampa, Idaho, and Carolyn, there were no other missionaries at the hospital after 1980. All the other staff members were Indian.

Soon after taking over as administrator of Reynolds Memorial Hospital in 1980, Carolyn realized her schedule was "chocablock," a word she used to describe the innumerable problems of staff and students who came through her office door. And even more perplexing was her realization that she was a white American sitting in a position of leadership telling brown Indians in their own country what to do. Before independence in 1947 perhaps that was acceptable, but Carolyn felt a little more uncomfortable with each day. She wondered how she would feel if the situation were reversed!

One day, after praying and asking God for wisdom, Carolyn shared her dilemma with a dear friend, Bamini Meshramkar, wife of Dr. K. J. Meshramkar, the medical superintendent at the hospital. When Carolyn related her feelings of frustration and discomfiture about doing her job, Bamini reached out and took Carolyn's hands and literally dragged Carolyn and herself to their knees.

"We will pray now," her friend said. "Lord,

just like You took Joseph, a foreign administrator, down to the country of Egypt, so You have brought Sister Myatt to us . . ."

Immediately Carolyn knew this was the Word of the Lord! She was familiar with the biblical account of how God had prepared and used the Israelite slave Joseph in a foreign land. However, the thought had never occurred to her that it had any parallel to her present position in India. This insight from a trusted friend brought tremendous peace.

In addition to Carolyn's administrative responsibilities at the hospital, she taught a full load of classes in the school of nursing. She taught pediatric nursing, a vital need in India where 42 percent of the population are children. These children were particularly vulnerable to many communicable diseases running rampant at the time, such as polio, tuberculosis, and leprosy. She also taught some of the subspecialties of medical-surgical nursing.

Then there was a need for someone to give anesthesia. This meant being available on the three days a week surgery was performed, as well as emergency call nights. Carolyn shared her anesthesia duties with three other nurses.

Carolyn's home was often referred to as the Myatt Regency. In rural Washim there were no adequate hotels, motels, or restaurants, so people coming to the hospital from other missions or from abroad were given room and board at her home. She normally did not keep a statistical record of hospitality events or guests; however, one year she decided to add this information to her annual report. She was surprised to learn she had served over 800 guest meals from January until August.

Another consistent dilemma Carolyn faced, amid her awesome responsibility and unrelenting workload, was this:

> How can I, as a member of an affluent society, minister to the poorest of the poor? How much should I change my way of living, eating, and dressing? Is it fair to have so much when the majority of my Indian colleagues and acquaintances have so little? Was Mother Teresa of Calcutta a model to follow? She gave up her citizenship, adopted a sari as her habit, slept on an iron bed with a thin mattress, and had a metal bucket in which to wash her clothes. Would my ministry be more fruitful if I changed my lifestyle?

God helped Carolyn work through that dilemma. She eventually concluded, "It may not be necessary for us to withdraw from home and friends," as F. D. Myers wrote, "but we shall have to withdraw our soul's deepest dependence upon all earthly props and support if we are to learn to trust simply and absolutely the eternal God."

7

Mountaintops and Valleys

"I took you from the ends of the earth, from its farthest corners I called you. I said, 'You are my servant'; I have chosen you and have not rejected you. So do not fear, for I am with you; do not be dismayed, for I am your God. I will strengthen you and help you; I will uphold you with my righteous right hand" (Isa. 41:9-10).

The 50th anniversary celebration of Reynolds Memorial Hospital in 1988 in the town of Washim in central India was only a pleasant memory. The 35 overseas guests from six countries had returned home. An impressive, engraved granite monolith—a tribute to honor Dr. Orpha Speicher, physician and founder of the hospital—was a new addition to the central courtyard. It represented not only her contribution but also the services of medical missionaries Jean Darling, Geraldine Chappell, Esther Howard, Hilda Moen, Dr. Don Miller, and Dr. Ira Cox, as well as Indians who had served alongside Dr. Speicher. The anniversary project, the computerization of the business office at the

The inner courtyard of Reynolds Memorial Hospital with a monolith honoring founder Dr. Orpha Speicher

hospital, was indeed a challenging and aggressive undertaking. There were no computers in Washim at the time—no Windows, no Google, not even telephone hookups!

Neither Carolyn nor any other person working at the hospital had ever used a computer. Even so, Carolyn knew the setup and follow-though of the computer installation would require many hours of her already full schedule as hospital administrator. In such a rural area it was impossible to attract and hire people who were computer literate. American College, a Christian institution in south India, had agreed to program and set up the computer system for the hospital. The professor in charge of the computer laboratories at the college cautioned Carolyn that the accuracy of the data that was submitted to them would determine how useful the computer would be to the hospital.

Carolyn began to gather data. The minute details of how each and every supply was ordered, delivered, stored, and finally distributed to patients had to be given to the programmers. Formulas had to be written for calculating financial transactions. Process and procedure questions of all sorts had to be answered: What were the criteria for giving free care to patients? How was staffing information maintained and stored? What was each employee's salary scale? How was overtime calculated? How were penalties for absenteeism assessed? The list of what, who, why, and how seemed endless. Carolyn found herself burning the midnight oil at home as well as in her office.

Carolyn had to intersperse her fact-finding mission with her other responsibilities. She continued to teach her nursing classes, solve administrative problems, and give anesthesia, as well as submit government-mandated documents and welcome hospital guests to her home. As chairperson of the Mid-India Board of Nurse Examiners (MIBE), she attended and chaired meetings. MIBE is the Christian organization recognized by the Indian government to grant diplomas to nursing students graduating from Christian nursing schools in middle and north India. These diplomas are registered by the government's Indian Nursing Council. Christian nurses from India serve around the world based on the registration of their diplomas.

In 1989 Carolyn went to her Himalayan retreat for her summer vacation. She was glad to have time away from work, but instead of using the time for rest and relaxation, she used it to write a Nazarene mission biography of Dr. Orpha Speicher, titled *A Tapestry Called Orpha*. When Carolyn returned to Washim, her older brother, Bill Beeler, arrived on an individual Work and Witness trip. He helped the hospital maintenance staff improve the water delivery system at the hospital. When Bill was leaving to return to the United States after six weeks, he said to Carolyn, "You are working too hard! You need to take more time for rest." Carolyn smiled, but she knew she had work at hand that would not wait.

Carolyn rarely had headaches, but more and more she suffered from both headaches and dizziness. On one trip to south India to consult on the progress of the computer, Carolyn was dizzy the entire time she was traveling. She was glad the hospital's business manager was a traveling companion. He took care of transferring their bedrolls, food baskets, and luggage at the six stations where they had to change trains.

When Carolyn's health did not improve, the hospital doctors insisted she get bed rest. Dr. Speicher, who was visiting India at the time and staying at Carolyn's home, was consulted. It was decided that Carolyn should return to the United States for diagnosis and treatment. Missionary colleague Joyce Jakobitz accompanied Carolyn on the trip.

Carolyn picks up the story from here:

> My brother and his wife, Evelyn, met me at the airport and took me to their home. My family doctor made an emergency appointment with a neurologist. This specialist assured me that he saw no signs that would indicate a brain tumor, but he said he wanted me to have an MRI, and it was scheduled. The doctor's staff asked me if I was claustrophobic

and I chuckled and assured them that I had never had any fear of closed spaces. However, when the MRI technician attempted to put my head inside the machine, I became terrified and shouted to the technician to take me out [of it]. It seemed like the MRI had become a coffin. I can never remember being as terrified as I was at that point. The staff scheduled a later appointment for me and told me I would be sedated for the procedure.

I slept fitfully that night, and when I awakened the next morning, I knew something drastic was happening within me emotionally. The fear I had experienced the previous day still consumed me, and all I could think about was how hopeless everything around me was. I could not eat and I cried a lot. It seemed I had descended into a deep, dark, scary place. The emotional pain was gut-wrenching!

Evelyn and Bill took me back to the family physician. He was surprised to see how deeply depressed I had become. I asked him to prescribe an antidepressant medication for me.

Although my emotional state improved from day to day, my family physician wanted me to see a psychologist. When I called the psychologist's office, I was told a Christian psychologist who had served as a missionary in Kenya was available to see me. What a blessing from God the man was to me. He understood the ramifications of cross-cultural living and obviously had great respect for me and for my Christian commitment.

In my talks with the psychologist I told him of my extremely heavy workload. I told him that I had managed to cover it all because I was a workaholic. At that time I thought that being a workaholic was a positive characteristic. His next question made me doubt my evaluation of that characteristic. "Do you know what drives you?" he asked. "Drives me?" I had to admit that I did not. At the end of that session he made a suggestion that I visit my other siblings if I had an opportunity.

That evening my younger brother Norman phoned me from Ohio and invited me to come for a visit. I accepted his invitation. Soon after I arrived, Norm handed me a book titled *Happiness Is a Choice*. The subject of the book was depression and was written by Christian psychiatrists Minirth and Meyer. The psychiatrists related that the people most prone to depression are people who deliver services to others—preachers, missionaries, doctors, nurses, and caregivers. I was greatly encouraged and challenged by the book. I asked my brother to take me to the bookstore so I could buy a copy for myself.

When we entered the bookstore, my brother pointed out the rack from which he had picked up his copy. I soon located a copy, and as I turned toward the cash register, I spotted another book on the same rack by the same authors titled *We Are Driven*. There was that word again—"driven"! That was the word the psychologist had used when he talked to me about my workaholic behavior. The book's information was like water to a very thirsty person. I began to see why and how I became burned-out.

I took antidepressant medication for only three months. When the medication was discontinued and I remained stable, I was cleared to return to India. However, before I returned I made a plan to delegate many of my responsibilities to others. I implemented that plan quickly.

I have been well since that initial episode. Nevertheless, I remember the horrific pain I suffered at that time and, therefore, want others to know there is a way out of that deep, dark valley. . . . I want Christians who question their own spirituality because they suffer from depression to know that God's grace kept me through that painful time in my life and He will do the same for them. His promise in Isaiah 41:10 to "strengthen and help us and to uphold us with His right hand" assured me then and assures me now.

8
The Right Choice

"We have a knack for ruining large chances
by very small choices" (Jeff Crosno).

When Carolyn returned to the United States on furlough in 1993, she seemed to be at the height of her usefulness as a global missionary in India. After serving there for 29 years she felt more Indian than American. She loved the Indian people, and the Indian people loved her. She was as comfortable in one of the many jewel-toned saris that had been given to her as gifts by her Indian friends as she was in a Western-style shirtwaist dress. Guests were delighted with the meals she prepared that were seasoned with hot, pungent curry spices that had been so troublesome when she first arrived in India. Moreover, a program Carolyn had envisioned and initiated as an outreach health ministry of Reynolds Memorial Hospital was changing the way health-care needs were met in underserved rural areas.

Carolyn and Hannah Howard, an MK from Papua New Guinea, in traditional Indian saris

The idea for the program began with Carolyn questioning whether institution-based health care (patient care centered on treatment at a hospital) was the best way to meet health needs in underserved areas. She attended the Jamkhed Rural Health Care Project—a workshop for community-based health care. In this workshop she saw illiterate Indian women become the health-care experts for their communities. These women taught villagers how to provide sanitation, clean water, midwifery, childcare, and other services.

Carolyn knew the curative approach to medical care was not the answer. It would get people healthy only to see them return to the same village and get sick again because the village itself was unhealthy. Carolyn came back from the workshop convinced that Reynolds Memorial must begin an outreach program. But she knew it could not happen unless the hospital staff embraced the concept. After several months the outreach ministry began.

The Community-Based Health Care project initially consisted of 10 villages in a radius of 10 miles of Reynolds Memorial Hospital, with a population of about 1,000 each. A project team from Reynolds Memorial traveled four times a week to these villages where there was no resident doctor, nurse, or health facility. In these villages this team accepted the challenge of training women, chosen by the village people themselves, to meet their basic health needs. These volunteers were the "doers." They helped immunize adults and chil-

Community-Based Health Care staff in a village setting in India

dren against tetanus, and children against diphtheria, whooping cough, and polio. Despite an intact caste system, all strata of society accepted these women.

Now in these villages, instead of premature death, there is life. Instead of sickness, there is health. Instead of despair and resignation, there is hope. But best of all, the project team introduced Christ to those who needed Him.

At the time Carolyn returned to the United States on furlough—before beginning her final four years before retiring—she was in an assignment where she seemed to find an outlet for all of her God-given talents. She was recognized as a compassionate nurse and gifted teacher of nursing, an efficient administrator, a beautiful soloist, an author, a mentor, and a cherished friend and confidant.

In June 1994, just three months before she was to return to India, Carolyn flew from her deputation assignment in Georgia to Nazarene Headquarters in Kansas City. While in Georgia she had been hospitalized for a severe malarial attack.

Carolyn was in Kansas City to give her report to church leaders of her work for the past four years. Over the years she had given many such reports to this group and it seemed like a routine thing. Instead, she was taken to a special room where she heard the startling announcement: "You will not be returning to India in September."

And there was more. These words meant to be an accolade resounded hollowly in her heart: "Inasmuch as Reynolds Memorial Hospital in India has been completely nationalized under your leadership, you have reached the epitome of missionary service. You have worked yourself out of a job."

Not returning to my beloved India! What do

they mean? Carolyn's heart was pounding and her mind was racing as she tried to grasp a possible explanation and the implications for this unfathomable turn of events.

There was more equally startling information to come: "You are being reassigned to Papua New Guinea so you can repeat in that country what you did so well in India. You are to start Community-Based Health Care there."

Give up India? Carolyn questioned silently. *How can I do that, and why do I have to? I have just one more term of missionary service before retiring, and I'm nearly 60 years old. Most of my friends live in India. My whole support system is there. Why do I have to go through the struggles of living and working in a new culture? At this age how can I possibly learn another language quickly enough to proceed with this mandate?*

Did she really want to learn a new language and make the tedious effort required to bond with a group of people evolving from a Stone Age culture? This was a country where an isolated group of people was found that had been identified in recent years in the *National Geographic Magazine* as "the last Stone Age Civilization."

"What could I possibly accomplish in four years?" Carolyn asked the Lord. *Maybe I should just retire at this point. Maybe I should just refuse the assignment and stay in the United States . . .* Her mind was racing furiously.

But what about my call? That was a question she had to ask herself. And when she did, she had to acknowledge that her call remained.

Is my call enough to take me to another country and sustain me while I serve there? That question was foremost in her mind when she left the United States for Papua New Guinea (PNG) in 1994. She had to make a stopover in India to pick up her belongings and say good-bye to all of her dear friends and colleagues.

"This stop in India will bring closure," was the reassurance she was given by friends when she left for India. However, reassurances do not always assure reality. The one month she spent in India was an emotionally rocky experience. Following a tearful farewell from her dear friends, Carolyn departed from India on October 20, 1994.

Carolyn flew to Singapore to connect with the flight that would take her to Papua New Guinea. She had a 14-hour layover in Singapore, so she booked a room in the airport rest area.

"I was physically and emotionally drained," Carolyn said. "And as I lay on the bed in that room, I thought, *I can't go on*. I begged God once again to release me from my call and allow me to return to my homeland. God was silent, so I traveled on to my new PNG assignment."

Some missionaries at her destination—the Nazarene Hospital at Kudjip—knew she was coming, but they did not understand fully what her assignment was to be. Despite having served 29 years in India, in PNG she felt very much like an absolutely new missionary recruit on her first assignment.

Carolyn began to search the Word for something that would speak to her. In the Scriptures she found a remarkably clear explanation of what God had in store for her.

Carolyn relates, "One day as I was searching the Word I came to a verse that spoke to me. It is located in Isaiah 43:18-19: 'Forget the former things; do not dwell on the past. See, I am doing a new thing! Now it springs up; do you not perceive it? I am making a way in the desert and streams in the wasteland.'"

"A new thing?" Carolyn asked the Lord.

"What is this new thing?" God soon began to show her what can happen when she, or anyone, totally relies on Him and is committed to His leadership and will.

9

A New Thing

"Pythagoras said that the most divine art is of healing. And if the healing art is most divine, it must occupy itself with the soul as well as with the body, for no creature can be sound as long as the higher part of it is sickly" (Apollonius of Tyr).

Soon after Carolyn arrived at the hospital in Kudjip, she was told there were no funds appropriated for the Community-Based Health Care program, but there was going to be a commission set up by the General Board of the Church of the Nazarene to study Nazarene Health Care Ministries in PNG. Perhaps the outcome of this commission would provide the answers to the questions about her assignment.

Within three months of Carolyn's arrival in PNG, members of the study commission met at Kudjip Hospital. At the end of the three-day meeting, her heart skipped a beat as she walked into the room where the group had gathered and saw written on the board: "Community-Based Health

Care will be the focus of Nazarene health ministries in Papua New Guinea." Wow, she was overwhelmed!

"We will continue the hospital," the commission reported, "and we will continue the school of nursing; however, Community-Based Health Care (CBHC) will be the focus of the health ministries in Papua New Guinea."

Appropriate changes were made to establish the new division of CBHC, but there were no funds to run the division and hire the staff. However, four months after Carolyn arrived, a German Christian funding agency agreed to honor a funding request made earlier by a former Kudjip missionary doctor. The request had been for an institutional model of primary health care. Carolyn questioned the wisdom of accepting the grant because she knew that if a CBHC program was to be successful, it must take place in communities where the people lived and not be a program attached to the hospital.

"Rewrite the project proposal any way you want. Just keep it within the amount we have set and you are free to use it for CBHC programs," the Germans replied.

Some of the Papua New Guinean staff of a CBHC birth attendant center where village women are trained as midwives

Amazingly, within four months of Carolyn's arrival in Papua New Guinea, funding for the project had gone from 0 to $250,000! In addition, God allowed nine of the very best PNG nurses to work with her in CBHC.

One of those nurses, Joseph Sika, had a miraculous story of grace to tell. Joseph was working in a Nazarene health center in Sangapi, which can only be reached by landing a small plane on a gravel airstrip on a mountainside. Carolyn radioed Joseph at Sangapi and asked if he would like to work in

CBHC. Joseph readily agreed to the transfer. He requested a car to meet him at the airport because he had been ill and was feeling very weak.

Carolyn met Joseph at the Mount Hagen airport and quickly discerned that being "very weak" was an obvious understatement. He was gaunt and coughing repeatedly. He acknowledged he had lost a lot of weight. Missionary physician Dr. Bob Merki diagnosed his problem as tuberculosis. Joseph was hospitalized and started receiving antitubercular medicine. After only four months of treatment Joseph's X ray was clear, and he was taken off all medication. God had healed him! Joseph's outstanding contribution to CBHC cannot be gauged. When Carolyn relinquished the directorship of CBHC to PNG nurse leadership, Joseph assisted Director Bernard Gunn and then went on to become the first PNG administrator to serve as director of Nazarene Health Ministries of PNG.

Carolyn knew she had only four years to get the program on its feet so it would not fail when she left the country. She also knew she needed people who understood the CBHC concept to take over leadership roles. So she asked for and received $9,000 in Compassionate Ministry funds to send Joseph and another nurse, Bernard Gunn, to India to study at the famous Jamkhed project. They both received diplomas in CBHC and, upon return, were ready to accept leadership in the Nazarene CBHC program.

In addition to the $250,000 from the Germans to run the program, God provided another $40,000 to build traditional PNG houses for the CBHC staff. Carolyn's home congregation at Washington, Pennsylvania, donated funds to purchase a photocopier. And when Carolyn and the team needed a vehicle to take them safely over the treacherous roads cut in the sides of steep mountain slopes that were often slick and muddy, God provided the money for a sturdy four-wheel drive. Most weeks brought more funds and gifts. The CBHC office became known as the Miracle-a-Day office.

Though Carolyn had never written a project proposal, she knew that if CBHC was to succeed, they had to have money from outside sources. Of necessity, she began to write grant proposals, very aware that God was giving her the skills to do it. By the time Carolyn left PNG, slightly less than 2 million dollars to run CBHC programs had been received or were in the pipeline.

God had said in His Word He would do a "new thing." The Community-Based Health Care program had begun because it was God's time. And it was God's program. It was more wonderful than anything Carolyn or anyone involved in the program could imagine.

When Carolyn arrived in PNG, she learned that 90 percent of the people lived in remote areas that were medically underserved. Many of those who needed medical care would have to walk for several days through the mountains to have access to someone who could fly them to a hospital from a makeshift airstrip. Many died on the way.

Carolyn and CBHC staff traveled to communities throughout PNG to train volunteers in preventative health care. These volunteers helped with such things as immunizations, healthy birth practices, monitoring the growth of babies, and environmental hygiene. These are vital health matters in Papua New Guinea, where 80 percent of the diseases are preventable through better hygiene.

By the time Carolyn left PNG, the CBHC program was being implemented in 22 communities. In those four-plus years, CBHC staff had trained approximately 1,000 people to deliver health care to their communities. The staff had trained men and women to become the health experts for their villages so the people would not have to trudge over those treacherous mountain passes to get medical help. They knew how to run the program, set priorities for the health care of their communities, be responsible for it, and take ownership for the deficiencies in their neighborhoods.

It is difficult to communicate how monumental the change was to be for the entire country. Even though the governmental leadership of PNG had gone a different direction in health care, it began to get interested in what was taking place in the bush communities in the Highlands. They called Bernard Gunn and Carolyn to the capitol in Port Moresby to help national leaders understand the Nazarene CBHC program.

Since then, advances in CBHC have been implemented in many of the PNG provinces (states), and the Nazarene program provides the model for the government of PNG to use for the entire nation. The government is using the Nazarene training manuals as the basis for their own training material. Some of the nurses who were trained by Carolyn, as well as current staff, help train government health workers through workshops and seminars.

Rural communities are being transformed and developed into healthy communities. The people themselves have taken responsibility for their own health care through disease prevention and development ventures. Infant and maternal mortality has fallen significantly in the areas where the CBHC models are being used.

Tribal customs and practices that have kept these communities impoverished and underdeveloped are being changed or eliminated. Bride-price, a custom that was originally used to bind two tribes together through marriage, has in some places disintegrated into a moneymaking affair. Now some communities regulate the custom so that they don't use funds that rob themselves of developmental opportunities. Some communities have decided to abolish the custom entirely.

In the beginning, the leaders of CBHC made the decision to move their offices away from the hospital at Kudjip to Kiam, where the district superintendent lived. This was not because of any lack of harmony between this new ministry and the hospital, but because the CBHC leaders felt their association with the Church of the Nazarene would facilitate their work with pastors. For Carolyn, ministering to spiritual needs was never an optional component to health care; it was the motivating force.

Carolyn emphasized from its conception that CBHC was to be a holistic ministry based on a spiritual dimension. She shared with the health-care workers being trained that if you are going to be healthy, you must be not only physically healthy but also at peace with yourself, at peace with others, and at peace with God. Thus she wanted CBHC to work with the churches.

Because of the CBHC training emphasis, the leaders of the program were required to be physically healthy themselves in body and spirit, and this in turn ensured the communities were being evangelized. Those 1,000 people who were the health-care volunteers were told to go back and revolutionize their neighborhoods. They became evangelists, presenting the Lord Jesus Christ. As these leaders trained individuals in their own community, the church became the focus of their work.

District Superintendent Andrew Akus in the first district established in Papua New Guinea told

Carolyn with CBHC staff at her farewell service in 1999

Carolyn: "Community-Based Health Care has become the greatest tool of evangelism the Church of the Nazarene has seen in the years since Wanda and Sydney Knox came into Papua New Guinea." And that was more than 50 years ago.

As Carolyn watched and experienced the unfolding of the CBHC program, she realized it was far beyond what she had ever thought or dreamed. It was a marvelous time in her life.

"When I think back to that time in the Singapore hotel and realize that I could have missed God's will for my life and the people of Papua

New Guinea," Carolyn says, "it stops me dead in my tracks. What if God had given me my wish? If the Lord had honored my self-serving wishes, what would have happened?

"When I went home to the United States for my final deputation, God spoke to me through these words in an article by Jeff Crosno, then pastor of the First Church of the Nazarene of Pasadena, California. In the June 1999 issue of the *Holiness Today* magazine he wrote:

> 'We have a knack for ruining large chances by very small choices. Our kinsman Esau threw away his birthright for a bowl of "red stuff." Certainly it was not the last time one of us has cost ourselves a future we cannot imagine to satisfy a hunger we cannot name.
>
> 'Or maybe you remember David. Not the young warrior musician after God's own heart, but the bored and jaded king who indulged himself with his neighbor's wife because he was sloppy where he spent his time. You may remember Peter, the confidant of Jesus who betrayed the Lord he loved, in no small part because he decided to sleep through prayer meeting. The biblical record is

consistent. It does not take much to lose a birthright, a kingdom, a Lord. The only requirement is insensitivity in small decisions and throw-away moments.'"

Carolyn related this teaching to her life like this: "My small choice not to go to Papua New Guinea that I requested in that Singapore hotel would have affected not only my life but also the lives of the people who are coming to the Lord through the ministry of Community-Based Health Care. When I went to Papua New Guinea, God said, 'I am going to do a new thing. Do you not perceive it?' Never in my wildest imagination could I have perceived all that He has done and is doing.

"I've served the Lord since I was 12," Carolyn confides, "but this was the first time I was able to look back and actually count people who would have been influenced for eternity, probably negatively, if I had persisted with my small choice.

"Each of us may affect the eternal destiny of others. Each of us may choose to be self-serving, rather than self-giving," she concludes. "Christ made the choice of being self-giving rather than self-serving. And we cannot escape the decision to do likewise."

Epilogue

"The steadfast love of the LORD never ceases,
his mercies never come to an end;
they are new every morning; great is
your faithfulness" (Lam. 3:22-23, NRSV).

After formal retirement in September 2000, Carolyn returned to Papua New Guinea the following March to complete the massive undertaking of publishing five training manuals for Community-Based Health Care workers. When this project was completed, the CBHC leaders honored Carolyn with a mumu—a traditional Papua New Guinean feast—and dedicated a beautiful memorial garden on the grounds of the Community-Based Health Care headquarters.

In 2006, Carolyn was honored with a Lifetime Achievement Award by her alma mater, Eastern Nazarene College.

Carolyn has continued to educate people in the CBHC concept. Since retiring she traveled to Guatemala City to attend the Nazarene Health Care Fellowship's Global Conference to speak about CBHC. She taught a CBHC course to a

Carolyn in retirement volunteering as a teacher's aid at Christian Central Academy in Houston, Pennsylvania

group of health-care professionals at the Asia-Pacific Nazarene Theological Seminary in the Philippines and traveled to Thailand to share the CBHC concept there.

Where does Carolyn call home now that she is retired? That is a testimony of God's faithfulness in itself. Few other than the Papua New Guineans who were coworkers at CBHC from the beginning knew that Carolyn had given a large gift from her retirement funds to build a house for the director of CBHC at Kiam. She did this thinking she would live in a missionary retirement center when she returned to the United States. But her brother Bill Beeler's wise investment and management of a small inheritance left when their mother passed away had accumulated funds for Carolyn to purchase a town house in Houston, Pennsylvania, near her older siblings, Marion, Doris, and Bill. At 65 years of age, she was able for the first time to have a home of her own and have the joy of furnishing it with the mementos she had collected in India and Papua New Guinea.

Carolyn enjoys her town house. However, you won't usually find her in a rocking chair on the deck enjoying the beauty of the flowers and meandering stream that flows nearby. Instead, she will be speaking at Faith Promise meetings, teaching an adult Sunday School class, serving as missionary-in-residence for summer camps, volunteering at a Christian elementary school as a teacher's aide, or in many other ways busy about the Lord's work. God's call has sustained her!

Pronunciation Guide

Chapter 3

Monongahela	moh-nah-GAH-hay-lah

Chapter 5

Balbodh	bahl-BOHD
Ki	KIE
Marathi	muh-RAH-tee
Salaam	saw-LAW-awm

Chapter 6

Bamini Meshramkar	baw-MIE-nie meh-SHRAWM-ker
Buldana	boul-DAW-naw
Nalini Yangad	naw-LEE-nee YAWN-gawd

Chapter 7

Moen	moh-EHN
Speicher	SPIE-ker

Chapter 9

Akus	AW-koos
Gunn	GEWN
Hagen	HAW-gen
Kiam	KEE-awm
Kudjip	KOO-juhp
Sangapi	suhn-GAW-pee